O. S. Barrett

Reminiscences, Incidents, Battles, Marches and Camp Life

Of the old 4th Michigan Infantry in War of Rebellion, 1861 to 1864

O. S. Barrett

Reminiscences, Incidents, Battles, Marches and Camp Life
Of the old 4th Michigan Infantry in War of Rebellion, 1861 to 1864

ISBN/EAN: 9783337116514

Printed in Europe, USA, Canada, Australia, Japan

Cover: Foto ©ninafisch / pixelio.de

More available books at **www.hansebooks.com**

REMINISCENCES, INCIDENTS, BATTLES,

MARCHES and CAMP LIFE

OF THE

OLD 4th MICHIGAN INFANTRY

IN WAR OF REBELLION,

1861 TO 1864.

By O. S. BARRETT,

LATE LIEUT. CO. B, 4TH MICHIGAN INFANTRY.

Dedicated to the Survivors of the Regiment.

Hope for the living,
Tears for the dead.

DETROIT, MICH.:
W. S. OSTLER, PUBLISHER,
1888.

THE

❈FOURTH ✦ REGIMENT❈

Michigan Volunteer Infantry

was organized at Adrian, Michigan, and Mustered into
United States Service June 20, 1861, for three years. It was
quartered in the North College building, of the group of
buildings situated at extreme west suburbs of City. Was
commanded by Dwight A. Woodbury. It was presented by
the ladies of Adrian, with a beautiful flag. The Regiment
left its Rendezvous June 25th, for Washington, numbering on
its rolls 1025, officers and men. In his orders for the movement, Colonel Woodbury said : "Let each man remember
that he has the honor of Michigan in his keeping." The first
appearance of the Regiment, while passing through Cleveland, Ohio, brought from the Leader of that city, the following notice of

MICHIGAN TROOPS.

"When we see the splendidly armed and equipped Regiments from Michigan, pass through here on their way to the
seat of war, and compare their appearance with that of the
Regiments that left Camp Cleveland recently, it makes us

almost ashamed of Ohio, and inclines us to enquire in the
mildest and most collected manner, why it is that Michigan
in the same length of time sends Regiments to the field pre-
pared for service, while Ohio, who boasts of her enterprise
and patriotism, sends from her camps as Regiments, mere
mobs of men, half uniformed, unarmed, and wholly without
drill."

The Regiment left Cleveland, via. Buffalo to Elmira,
New York, where we took supper with 23d New York Regiment in barracks there   We were royally entertained ; had
a good time : had a good supper.   I wish to say here, the
first hard tack the writer ever saw was issued to us at Cleveland.   They were round, and as large as an elephant's foot,
and as tough as a prohibitionist's conscience.   I noticed some
of the boys, out on platform of cars, trying how far they
could sail them.   Others had coupling pins, trying to pulver-
ize them.   On leaving Elmira, some of the boys who were a
little off, pulled the coupling pin, which detached three or
four cars.   The rest of the train pulled out some distance
before it was discovered.   The advance section backed up,
the rear cars were hitched on, and the boys were induced to
all-aboard, and the train passed on to Harrisburg, Pa.   The
Regiment encamped a few days at that city, and we were
drilled in the art of street fighting, expecting a collision at
Baltimore.   The people of Harrisburg asked : "has Michigan
sent another Regiment equipped ?"   And in fact the troops
at Camp Curtin "thought if Pennsylvania would only clothe
her men like that, she would not have a single citizen at
home."

From Harrisburg, on to Baltimore.   The Regiment was
disembarked from the cars some distance outside of the city ;
formed and marched into the depot.   We were armed with
old buck and ball muskets, and were not allowed but three
rounds of cartridges.   The Regiment was formed into pla-

roons, and marched through the general thoroughfare to Washington Depot. On its way, while about midway, the crowd was immense on the sidewalks, a demonstration was made by some crank of a Rebel, at a point opposite our colors, pointing a revolver toward the flag-bearer, but was suppressed so quick that it was not seen but by few of the Regiment. The writer was a file-closer and in rear of rear platoon, and saw the movement. Had that pistol been discharged, the result would have been a terrible indiscriminate slaughter. My gun was on a line with the act in less time than it would take to pull a trigger. Somebody would have been hurt. Men hissed and jeered, but the column moved on to Washington Depot, where the Regiment was embarked on cars for Washington. Just before reaching the Relay House, the train was stopped and we were told that Rebels were in our front. We were formed in line of battle. It was a false alarm. We got aboard again, and passed on to Washington. Arrived in that city on the night of July 2d, and soon went into camp on Meridian Hill, near Soldiers' Home. Remained in camp until a short time before first battle of Bull Run. The Regiment was ordered over the Potomac, and to Alexandria, and out to a place called Cloud's Mills. Remained in camp there, and done picket duty until a few days prior to first Bull Run, when it was ordered on to Fairfax Station, in rear of advancing army. The left wing of the Regiment was detained at that place, while the right was marched to Fairfax Court House. The writer was with the part remaining at the station. It was evident that the Rebels had left in a hurry, as the advance of our column appeared; they had tried to burn the station and other property, but were prevented by stress of time. We found plenty of corn meal ; also a number of hogs that had been corralled in the rear of the station, but had been let out of the pen ; on arrival of our men in pursuit, they were running around loose. The writer fired six shots at an old hump-backed sow, and got nary a swine. One W. W. Carpenter, the liliputian of Company B, killed her with one shot from an old Colt's revolver. We had mush and fresh pork in abundance. We found some cows on an abandoned plantation, near by. Also plenty of honey. We had mush and milk 'till you couldn't rest. One of the boys, while reconnoitering around, developed a colony of bees. He seized a hive and started for a brook near by. He attempted to jump a pole fence. His toe caught and he pitched headlong. The hive flew twenty feet. The bees followed back, and swarmed in his bushy hair, which caused a lively rush for the water. He plunged in and soon divested himself of the vicious little insects. But not daunted he returned, and seized the hive again. This time he succeeded in drowning the bees. He got the honey all the same. That night, after the adventure with the bees, myself and my bunkey tore some of the hives to pieces, and placed the boards on the ground, and spread our blankets on them for our bed. We went to bed tickled with our layout. About twelve o'clock we were aroused with injunction to keep very still, as Rebels were near, and were expected to attack us. My bunkey and I got up, or sat up. About that time I saw bunkey slap his legs, and heard him swear.

About the same time, I felt an unusal sensation under my pants, in the region of where I sat down. There were plenty of live bees still, that had staid with the boards. They had crawled inside our clothes, and everlastingly stuck it to us. Well, if you ever saw an Indian war dance, picture to yourself our appearance. We were ordered to keep still; but had a Brigade of Rebels attacked us, we would have fought these bees.

Next day was fought the first Battle Bull Run. We were ordered to join the other wing of the Regiment, at Fairfax Court House, arriving just before the stragglers began to appear from our defeated army. We were formed in the road, in sections, and ordered to stop all stragglers. Talk of stopping a cyclone; it was impossible. The rush of soldiers, congressmen, and other civillians, from Washington, literally forced us from the highway. I saw three officers on one mule, hatless, coatless, and unarmed, and apparently badly frightened; the Johnnies did not follow up with any force. The 4th was soon on the way to Washington. We returned to our old camp, on Meridian Hill. Early in fall of '61, the Regiment built fort Woodbury, on Arlington, and done picket duty. Later on, we were moved out to Minor's Hill, Virginia, and built winter quarters, and remained there during the winter 1861-2. The Regiment, with 14th New York, 9th Massachusetts, and 62nd Pennsylvania, formed 2d Brigade, 1st Division, 5th Army Corps, commanded by Fitz John Porter, a brave and skilfull officer, who was afterwards much abused ; for I believe we had no more loyal officer in the field ; to the contrary notwithstanding, his traducers tried to drag him down. Nothing of a startling nature occurred here, during the winter. Our time was occupied in picket, camp, guard, and other routine work. A laughable incident occurred here in camp, which illustrates the desire of the common soldier

FOR FUN AND FROLIC.

We were armed with the old Buck and Ball musket, which we were to exchange for the Enfield rifles. Word was given to the different companies to send details for guns. The Company B detail was dispatched. Soon the boxes were brought, and opened. Behold a mistake had been made, and the boys thought on purpose Instead of the Enfield, the boxes contained the same kind of guns we already had. The men were indignant, and refused to accept them, but finally concluded to use them awhile, as they were new and bright. The guns were distributed, and boxes ordered back, a procession formed a la funeral. An escort, with reversed guns, and music, and every conceivable thing that any noise could be got out of, followed to Quarter master's depot. A volley was fired over the boxes, and the procession returned to quarters. Soon, a racket was heard in vicinity of company B. Every other man had a gun sling around his body, and was down on all-fours. The other fellows had a gun thrust between the gun-sling and along the man's spine, firing blank cartridges. As soon as the gun was fired, the man on the

ground would assume a sitting posture, with the muzzle up. Then the gunner would ram cartridge, and the gun would immediately assume the horizontal, again to be fired. There were some 40 of the company engaged in this. That night, after the racket, the 14th New York's Sutler lost a barrel of whiskey, rolled out from under his tent early in the evening, while the proprietor was engaged in front with a special delegation sent to occupy him and his assistants, while the feat was being performed. It never was found, but you could buy a canteen-full for $5.00 of one who knew where it was. Details were made to hunt for it, but it was never brought to view, but some of the detail were quite drunk when they returned. I will relate an incident that occurred while encamped on Arlington, as stated before in this narrative: while stationed there, we were daily beset by hucksters and traffickers. They would vend their wares to the boys, and go away, apparently happy, but soon return again, seeming to be dissatisfied with what they received for their goods. One day, a pompous Jew drove over from Georgetown, a big wagon-load of goods drawn by four-in-

hand Sales were small until he struck company B, the writer's company. Here he cried his wares. Finally a syndicate was formed, and approached the vender of goods, with the proposition to buy his entire stock. They would give so much, provided he had a certain amount of the ardent in his outfit. He seemed to be satisfied with the situation, and answered, he had what they desired. The bargain was closed, and money paid in bills. Our goods were unloaded, and he departed, highly elated. But it was not long. He soon returned, alone, and inquired of the writer for the Colonel's tent. The writer edged around, as near as possible, to hear what was said. The Jew was swinging his arms, and gesticulating fiercely. The Colonel listened until he got through, then I heard him say, in reply, "you ought to be satisfied with small profits on so large a sale." He replied: "Colonel, the monish is not good, it is one Erie and Kalamazoo monish." The Colonel told him the result was as good as the intent, and dismissed him, and we did not see him again. The boys bought him out slick and clean, for 600 dollars, and paid him in new and crisp Michigan Insurance and older bills of Erie and Kalamazoo. I will say, Company B, was made up of one or two doctors, as many lawyers, and one preacher, and the rest were gentlemen. The writer was identified with the latter class.

THE REGIMENT MOVED.

With the advance of the army from Miner's Hill, and to Fairfax, passed beyond that dilapidated and dingy looking town, historical, much speculation indulged in, in regard to what route would be adopted "On to Richmond." It was finally decided to take the route via Alexandria down the Potomac to Fort Monroe. Accordingly, the columns were put in motion, and in due time the army arrived at above named place. Our Division passed out beyond Hampton, and went into camp, for a few days, then marched en route to Yorktown, by way of Big Bethel. On our arrival within cannon shot of Rebel fortifications, we were greeted by a general shower of shot and shell, from Rebel Batteries, which went screeching and screaming over our heads. The 4th had the advance at the right, toward the Rebel Left. As we drew nearer, they got our range. Their shot plunged and shells burst in and all around us with but little damage, but made the situation decidedly unpleasant. Our column filed to the right, following a ravine, which extended to extreme left of Rebel Earthworks. General Charles Griffin commanded our Division, and his old battery was on hand, that he had formerly commanded. He immediately ordered it to the front, out in open space, and commenced shelling the Rebel works. Cannonading was lively for a while, on both sides. The Rebels evidently misunderstood the demonstrations, so audaciously made in their front, and expected an immediate assault all along the line. They apparently reserved their fire for closer work, but were disappointed in that. The army settled down to a siege. We were constantly under fire, from time of arrival in front of their works, until evacuation of same, on picket line, bivouac and skirmishing. No let up night and day. Casualties were quite frequent. If a picket guard showed his head it was a target as soon as seen. Picketing was extremely dangerous business. The guard were posted under darkness of night and was relieved the same. In front of Rebel works was an open plain. The boys would dig holes, under cover of darkness, and through the day would burrow like gophers. Hence gopher holes, had dirt piled up in front with a hole at base, for to shoot through. Was death to the man who got his cranium above the obstruction in front of him. A thrilling incident occurred at this time. General Fitz John Porter, who commanded the 5th corps, went up in a balloon to take observations of rebel works. It was controlled by ropes, held by men on the ground. After getting up the right distance, the guy became detached, through some cause, and the balloon floated at will. first over Rebs, then back on our side, swayed by the wind. All this while, Porter could be seen standing up in the car,

with spy glass in hand, scanning the Rebel fortifications; and
the Johnnies everlastingly yelling, and trying to elevate their
guns to reach him, but failed. The elevation was too steep
for their gunnery. Finally he descended to our side, amid
shouts of the whole army. It was hard telling at one time
into what hands he would fall. The siege went on. A heavy
water battery of one hundred pounders was placed on York
River, at the extreme left of Rebel works. The 4th was
stationed at that point. These guns were worked spasmodi-
cally. Rebs could not reply to them. York River, at this
doint, was full of oysters—some the largest I ever saw. We
often went in after a supply. It was dangerous business.
The Rebel pickets, on opposite side, were alert and invariably
fired on any one who had the hardihood to approach the
water for them. The writer ventured in one day for some of
the bivalves, and was industriously searching for the precious
article. I succeeded in exhuming a monster big one, and
was looking for more, when zip, pinge, come the warning to
get out. I was in such a hurry I forgot to take along my
find, and you could not see my coat-tail for the water splash-
ing behind me. I did not want any more oysters on that
special occasion. Yorktown was evacuated on the night of
May 4th and 5th, 1862; our army had been to vast labor, and
the government to tremendous expense and worry. A bloody
battle was fought at Williamsburg; the 4th were not engaged
at that battle. We were sent via West Point, and followed
on to Chickahominy. The time occupied between Yorktown
and our arrival at the Chickahominy, was marching, and
camping under great hardships; mud and heat had to be con-
tended with. When within a few miles of Chickahominy,
the 4th was detached from the column, and in a pouring rain,
were hustled on to the river. When within half a mile of it
we met a squadron of cavalry, which had been to the point,
came back full well. We were ordered, "Battalion into line,

double quick;" my company being on the left, did some tall
running over bogs, ditches and small brush, to get our place
in line. We struck the river at New Bridge, and met a sharp
fire from opposite side. We were dressed up under this fire.
Our first man was killed here, a. m., D. Piper, of Company
B. He was shot dead. He was the largest man in the company. I was first sergeant at the time, and touched elbows
with him when he fell. The boys named him Elephant, on
account of his immense size. Our Colonel, D. A. Woodbury,
seeing our disadvantage, rode his horse down to the river and
ordered us to cross. At this time the Johnnies were seen to
get to the woods beyond. About 20th of May my company
plunged into the water, arm-pits deep. Company A crossed
over to the right, in a bend of the river. We found 28 dead
rebels in our immediate front. We brought over some
wounded rebels, and on our return the water was chin deep
to the writer, it having rained all this time heavily. There
were four or five of my company wounded. The rebels had
taken the plank from the bridge, and ranged two pieces of
cannon on the same. We held this point as a picket line
until battle of Gains Mills. The crossing of Chickahominy
occurred on May 24th, 1862.

Here I first saw Custer. He was sent by McClellan to as-
sist our cavalry in conducting the establishment of picket
lines at New Bridge. He crossed the river four times, on
horseback, to my certain knowledge. He encouraged us boys
with the example, and his cheering remarks, such as go in
Wolverines, give them h--l, and we did. The Johnnies out-
numbered us six to one, but they were deceived in our
strength, supposing us to be a regular advance of our army.
I am pained to read of the deprecating language of Major
Reno, 7th Regiment Cavalry, in regard to the gallant Custer.

This fight caused General McClellan to dispatch to the
War Department, the following : "Three skirmishes to-day.

We drove the Rebels from Mechanicsville, seven miles from New Bridges. The 4th Michigan about used up the Lousiana Tigers. Fifty prisoners, and fifty killed and wounded."

Mr. Greeley, in his American Conflict, says: "The first collision on the Chickahominy, between the advance of McClellan's army and the Rebels, occurred near New Bridge, where the 4th Michigan, Colonel Woodbury, waded the stream and assaulted and drove off a superior force, losing but eight men in all, and taking thirty-seven prisoners, of whom fifteen were wounded." After establishing line of pickets on or along the river, the regiment went into camp on Gains' Farm, on left bank of Chickahominy, about one mile from river. Soon after, the battle of Fair Oaks was fought in plain sight of our camp. It continued 'till early in the evening. We could see the flash of bursting shells and vomiting cannon. The excitement among the men of the regiment was very manifest. It is certainly pleasanter, at a distance, to witness a battle, than to participate in one. Distance is more agreeable than being too intimate with the struggle.

An advance from our position, at that time, was contemplated upon Richmond. A heavy rainstorm was raging at the time. The regiment stood in ranks all one day, in this rain—so did the whole army—waiting orders to cross the Chickahominy. The flats each side of the river were flooded from two to four feet deep. Whirling and seething in its course, it was impossible to cross, and had to be abandoned. A howl went up all over the north, because of the failure, but was not attributed to the high water, but to cautiousness or cowardice of the commander. It could not be done in the face of such difficulties. If ever there was an interposition of Providence, it was manifested at that time, for if we had crossed the river with the view of attacking Richmond, I believe the Army of the Potomac would have ceased to exist as an organization. Picketing and camp routine was daily gone through with at this time ; but little excitement, and nothing startling occurred. I think, May 27th, a column was marched to Hanover Court House to our right and rear. It was reported the Rebels were threatening our base. The 4th Regiment was a part of the troops composing that movement. We marched to Hanover. The front and rear of the column had a fight with the Johnnies. The 4th was but slightly en-gaged. The 9th Masschusetts, one of our brigade, had a lively chase after the enemy,—charged them out of a piece of woods, and down a grade, towards a railroad, via Hanover and Richmond. The 44th New York were badly cut up, being the regiment in the rear of the column that the Rebesl attacked with great fury. The 44th stood their ground with great bravery and determination until assistance arrived. The enemy was driven off, and the column returned to camp. Company B, of the 4th, acted as flankers on the return to camp, 14 miles away. By the way, the duties of flankers are very tedious and arduous. especially over a rough country, and is attended with a good deal of danger. On our way back, when near camp, the regiment halted in the road, with low hanging trees on one side of the road (the flankers had been called in,) with thick underbush. Some telegraph wires were laying along on the limbs. Some mischievious fellow in the rear drummed with his gun on them, causing a vibration of sound similar to a noise caused by a charging mule team running away. The result was, the road was vacated in two seconds. The writer jumped, and supposed he was jumping up grade, but instead, jumped 20 feet down grade, into a hole. The scare was over, and the column soon made camp. Many lost their caps, the writer among the rest. I distinctly saw the colonel and adjutant's horses leap a ditch fence on the north side of the road. If I could have known the fellow who caused the stampede, I think I could have mauled him

—and think I would, had I caught him. As it is, the friction is now worn off, and he is safe. I will say, the column was marching left in front. That put the writer's company to the front. Hence the scare at our end of the regiment. The army indulged in a grand review at this place. General Prim, the Spanish Patriot, was present, and, I think, President Lincoln, but am not positive as to the latter being present. The little general humped around after Mac., who was a splendid rider—none were more accomplished than Little Mac. Prim was not used to such rough ground and hard riding, hence his unsteady seat. While in camp, our quartermaster thought to regale us with the luxury of dried apple pies, shortened with bacon grease. He had procured a portable oven, and dispensed his goodies to the boys, at twenty five cents a small section. The writer remembers of being very sick from eating pie, in fact, the only time he remembers of being sick, until subsequently, after being wounded at Gettysburg.

And now comes the tug of war. Up to this time the regiment had not suffered very serious loss. True, many were sick ; some had been discharged ; but the regiment showed a good front. The history, from June 26th, 1862, of the regiment, is steeped in blood, with heavy loss. Many were sent to their last muster out, and now, after the lapse of a quarter of a century, the roster is nearly closed.

June 26th, 1862, the regiment, with the rest of the brigade, was formed in column, and marched out to Mechanicsville, and engaged in battle with traitors to this good country. The battle was short and sharp, without much advantage to either side. It was the prelude to one of the bloodiest battles of the war,—Gains' Mill. June 27th, 1862, the regiment, with others, left our camp, abandoned everything except our knapsacks and guns, marched out and formed line of battle, near Gains' Mill. The Rebels soon took possession of our deserted camp, rioted awhile on what was left,—whiskey, hard-tack, and other commodities. About ten A. M. they came down on us without skirmishers, with guns at a right shoulder arms, and drunk. They came to be slaughtered, and they got it, then and there. The carnage was terrible. The battle raged all day, until dark. Men, of human form divine, became demons, fought like wild beasts, and with not much more intelligence on the traitors' side. Many of the regiment went down.

The next day, loved ones, true as steel, were missing, and never again answered to human roll call. And on to other battles, the regiment was baptised in blood again. Savage Station, White Oak Swamp, and on to Malvern On the 30th of June, the army arrived at Malvern Hill, tired, worn, and hungry. The enemy followed up and attacked in the afternoon, but were easily repulsed. July 1st was the climax of battles. The enemy attacked with great fury; the battle raged all day with great slaughter, on both sides. Charge after charge was indulged in by the persistent foe, to be hurled back bleeding in every form. The thunder of cannon was awful; clash of arms, shouts of combatants, was deafening. Such a seething hell will never be again enacted on this continent. It would be impossible to repeat it, in all its details. The enemy drew off, and the Army of the Potomac passed on to Harrison's Landing, on the James River. The regiment lost its brave Colonel Dwight A. Woodbury, the bravest of the brave. His last words were, "hold them, boys." He was shot in the forehead and died almost instantly. His body now rests in our beautiful Oak Wood Cemetery. He was a kind man. The enemy followed to Harrison's Landing in small force; made a slight attack on our forces, on the morning of July 2nd, but we easily repulsed. The regiment and army settled down to camp life. While here, the Rebels made a night attack, from south side James River. Our heavy batteries and gun boats in the river soon knocked them out of the box. The day following, the 4th and 16th Michigan were ferried over the river to see about it. Found debris of caissons, dead horses, and evidence of demoralization. Staid over all day. Some captures were made. Among the trophies, were a considerable amount of geese. The regiments returned to north bank of stream and went into camp. The rebels did not attack again. The severe handling they received at their nocturnal demonstration evidently satisfied them. After the death of Colonel Woodbury, Lt. Col. Childs was promoted to Colonel of the 4th regiment; Lt. Col. Duffield was promoted to Colonel of 9th Michigan Infantry. After the Peninsular campaign had ended, the 4th returned, with the army, and entered on the "Pope Campaign." The regiment in command of Col. Childs was in the engagement at Gainsville, Aug. 29, 1862; Bull Run, Aug. 30, and at Antietam Sept. 17 following. At Shepardstown Ford, Sept. 20 with its brigade, it forded the Potomac, in face of a battery, killed and drove off the enemy, captured their guns. After the Maryland campaign, the regiment returned to the Potomac, and was in battle of Fredericksburg, Dec. 13th and 14th, 1862. Lt. Col. George W. Lumbard, commanded. Its loss in these two days was 9 killed, 41 wounded, and one missing; Lieut. James Clark was killed, Company B. Remember the 4th was always identified with 2nd brigade, 1st division, 5th corps, and was in said organizations until expiration of service. After battle of Fredericksburg, Dec. 13, 14, the 4th returned to north bank Rappahannock; on the 30th and 31st of December the regiment was engaged in a reconnoisance to Morrisville, making a march of 33 miles on the latter day. It was engaged in a movement on the 20th of January, 1863, marching only a few miles; returned to camp near Falmouth, where we remained until May 1st, sending out details, building corduroy roads, bridges, and other preparations, clearing the way for an advance to Chancellorsville. May 2d, it forded the Rapidan River, without opposition. On the 3d it marched out to and beyond Chancellorville, proper, and formed the extreme left of the army, 1st division, 5th corps. The division was cut off from the rest of its corps, at this time. We manouvered around, for a while. Finally it was decided to try and support the brave Sedgwick, commanding 6th corps, who was battling with the Johnnies at Fredericksburg. The column was put in motion, left in front, 4th Michigan in the lead—the writer's Company out as flankers. We soon heard the familiar Rebel yell, in our front. It put a stop to the movement. We returned, sadder but wiser, to our former position. It was then getting dark. The Division was put in motion to the rear, towards the bluffy ground near the Rappahannock River, where we were put in line of battle— our right extending towards Chancellorsville, our left near the river. It was high ground, and we considered it impregnable. The regiment, and in fact, the whole line, threw up temporary breastworks. In this position we passed the night of the 3d. Saturday, during the night, the 11th corps had stampeded, at Chancellorsville, and took to the woods, in rear, and could not be induced to return to the front. Sunday morning the sun rose clear and hot.

We received orders to march to the vacated position that had been occupied by the 11th corps. We double-quicked the entire distance, over rough ground. The underbrush had been cleared away partially. When we arrived in open space, where the fight was going on, we were quickly formed in echelon, battle array by division front. The Johnnies come out of the woods in our front with the apparent determination to drive us back; but grape and canister, accompanied by musketry, drove them back. They did not appear again that day. This was May 4th. The enemy contented themselves with annoying us with their sharpshooters, located in trees. in woods. in our front. Our officers concluded to teach them better manners than to kill men in this quiet and barbarous way. Accordingly, orders were given to deploy the 4th Michigan as skirmishers, and clear the wood, which was done in fine style, and at a double quick. I saw a rebel sharp-shooter, located in a tree some sixty feet from the ground, he had a telescope rifle, and on his head an old plug hat. He was shot, and came tumbling to the earth. He struck the ground straight out. He looked to be nine feet long, in his descent to the ground.

The line swept on, driving all before it. We soon struck Rebel works, composed of logs. In front was a ravine. As the Johnnys went up the incline, and over the works, we landed in the ravine. This saved us, as they could not fire to any advantage, while their men were ready to break their necks to get out of our way. They fired a tremendous volley over our heads ; our bugle sounded the "recall," and then we proceeded to "git"—"the Devil take the hindermost." Now, I was considered a smart runner, but could not gain an inch on the man ahead of me. On we went. We could hear the swish of cannister in our rear, but on we went. The 9th Massachusetts was sent after us as a support. It had halted half way and laid down. We passed over them in our flight. The Rebels soon followed up, and when in range of the guns of the 9th, they arose, and delivered their fire, which sent the survivors flying to their works. Thus ended the most exciting race of my life. I never shall forget it. It was amusing to. Colonel Welch, of the 16th Michigan, felt slighted because his Regiment was not selected for the job. I told him I was sorry, as I was willing he should have all the honor that would accrue to me. I was not very proud of such chances.

The army withdrew to the north bank of the Rappahannock. The 4th Michigan, 14th New York, 9th Massachusetts, 62d Pennsylvania, composing 2d Brigade, was rear guard to the United States Ford. The army moved in the night, leaving picket line established. Many were captured. After crossing the river, we encountered a sea of mud. The army slashed around until it arrived at our old camp at Falmouth. The 4th was camped at Stoneman's Switch. We remained there until May 26th, when it, the 4th, was ordered to Kelley's Ford, for guard duty, where it remained until the 13th of June, 1863. Here a laughable thing happened. The Johnnys were on one side of the river, and we occupied the other, doing picket; a long, lankey Johnny sat on the bank of the stream, poorly dressed, with his feet in the water; no firing at this time, by mutual consent. One of our smart Alicks sung out to him. "I say, Johnney Reb., why don't you wear better clothes?" His reply was prompt, "We uns don't wear our best clothes when we go to kill hogs." Our Alick subsided. This man was shot soon after. It was a cowardly deed. The Regiment participated in the long and fatigueing march to Gettysburg, Pennsylvania. On the way, at Aldie and Middleburg, it was detained in support of cavalry.

We passed on and across the Potomac ferry, at Edwards. On the way we saw plenty of evidence of the cavalry advance,—dead horses, accoutrements belonging to cavalry out-fit. We arrived at Hanover, Pennsylvania, on the afternoon of July 1st. Rested and fed ; then on to Gettysburg. Marched all night—a beautifull moon-light night. As we passed farm houses, the people came out with water and refreshments, handed us as we passed along foot-sore and tired. An Aide-de-camp came riding along, saying : "Boys, keep good courage, McClellan is in command of the army, again." Instantly the space above was filled with the hats and caps of the gratified soldiers. They shouted and hollered, and kicked up their heels, and were frisky with the supposed good news. I mention this to show with what veneration Little Mac. was held by the Army of the Potomac. I knew this was untrue, myself, but it served its purpose, as intended. Many a brave heart went down next day with that belief in his heart. On to Gettysburg. We arrived in sight of line of battle being formed, at 9 A. M., July 2nd. Lunched, and was then moved up near Round Top. Was halted again, and awaited the coming struggle. It came.

The regiment was formed in line of battle, with the brigade, and was moved nearer the battle going on in front of us, with other troops engaged. The regiment stood under fire at least a half hour before it became engaged, getting a large share of spent balls from the front. Soon the general commanding Division, Brown, said : " Boys, I want you to put in a few licks for Pennsylvania ; the Buck-tails will go in on your left. Forward." It was a relief to hear the order, " March." We advanced into the maelstrom of Rebel bullets. By some oversight our right was exposed, and we had to contend with three to one. We held them until they made a fierce charge, charging our right and doubling it to the rear of our left. We were taken at a great disadvantage. I looked to our rear ; our colors were there, and men rallying around them. Our colonel, H. H. Jeffords, was there, in the thickest of the struggle, calling on the boys to save the flag. They needed no urging ; they fought like demons. Our colonel was killed—shot and then bayoneted. A brave man was killed by the hand of a traitor,—and many others, too, who were simple privates, but heroes for all that ; every one of them who fell doing his duty, or imposed duty.

We had to fall back. The writer was here wounded, and the battle surged beyond him. Soon the enemy came, tearing back in retreat. They had struck the brave old 6th Army Corps, just arrived, and in time to save the day. The Rebels went back flying, with the 6th Corps men close after them.

They had no time to scoop any of the wounded, as they had all they could attend to in getting out themselves. It was now dusk; the fierce struggle was over for the night. The struggle had been simply terrible; the carnage was awful; the fire incessant. Groans and oaths of the wounded were heard on every hand. Many would have recovered, had they had care. But it was impossible to reach all. The writer, with others, was loaded into an ambulance, at two o'clock in the morning of July 3d, and taken to an old house to the north, and east of the battle ground. Here were many wounded. Among those in the house was a Rebel Colonel, shot through the breast. He sat in the only chair in the house. He commanded a Louisiana Regiment, and was wounded early in the fight. I saw him lying on the ground, after the fight had surged by me. I think he died.

The 2d day of July, 1863, ended the writer's service in the field. The 3d day of July was ushered in with an ominous quiet. No sound of cannon broke the stillness, until near ten o'clock, A. M., when mutterings of the awful srife, inaugurated later, began to be heard. Soon the din began. The voices of an hundred big mouthed guns began to vomit forth its death dealing missiles. The Infantry now began to put in its refrain; after a few spasmodic belchings, of the firing, the tremendous concussion of all arms became general. About five miles of line of battle could be seen from where us non-combatants lay. The whole line was ablaze. Firing was incessant. Salvos after salvos, of artillery belched forth. The air was full of flying missiles—death everywhere. Thus the strife continued all day—an awful day, too, for those who lay helpless in plain view. Charge after charge was made by the determined enemy, but they were repulsed each and every time by the boys in blue. The anxiety was terrible to those who could not participate in the struggle. The very air seemed to be ablaze. The suspense became painful later in the day. Such persistency seemed, must be, rewarded with success.

Still the fight went on, and seemed to us an age of suspense. Many wounded came from the front. Ten thousand questions were asked of those who had been wounded, "how goes the battle?" Some would answer, doubtful, others would say, "our side would win." It was curious to note the countenances of those who heard the news, some with great anxiety in their faces, others with confidence depicted in every feature. Finally, the awful noise died away; news was brought by an aid-de-camp "that the enemy had hauled off." These men who were dying would raise themselves to a sitting posture, and utter one hurrah! Lay down and die! The work of death ceased. The rebels retreated. Thus ended the three days battle of Gettysburg The 4th ranks were badly depleted. So was the whole army. The sanitary commission was on hand, and rendered great service, in the care of the wounded. One poor fellow of our regiment, a company D man, was shot in the head. He would get on his knees, put his head on the ground, and twist his head in the ground. He bored that way until death put an end to his sufferings. Many died of their wounds, and were buried then and there. The wounded were sent away as fast as possible. The writer, with others, left for Baltimore, and remained a few days at that place, at a Catholic Infirmary. We were treated with great kindness by the Sisters of that benevolent institution. The ladies of Baltimore—God bless them—they regaled us with all the luxuries of the season, I can never forget their kindness.

The subsequent history of the regiment is taken from the official sources, (Michigan in the War,) with some personal recollections.

The struggle in which the regiment was engaged at Gettysburg, may be inferred from the following notice of the services of its corps, the 5th, as stated by Mr. Greeley, in his "American Conflict." Sickles new position was commanded by the Rebel Batteries, posted on Seminary Ridge, in his front, scarcely half a mile distant. While magnificent lines of battle, a mile and a half long, swept up to his front and flanks, crushing him back with heavy loss, and struggling desperately to seize Round Top, at his left. Meade, regarded this hill as vital to the maintenance of our position, and had already ordered Sykes, to advance the 5th corps, with all possible haste, to save and hold it.

A fierce and bloody struggle ensued, for the enemy had nearly carried the hill before Sykes reached it. While Humphrey, who with one of Sykes' Divisions, had been posted on Sickles' right, was in turn assailed in front and flank, and driven back with a loss of 2,000 out of 5,000 men.

After the death of Colonel Jeffords, Lt. Col. Lumbard assumed command of the Regiment, pursuing the enemy from Gettysburg; the 4th marched to Williamsport. On July 12th, the enemy having crossed the Potomac, the Regiment proceeded to Berlin; thence on the 17th it marched to Warrenton, by way of Mannassus Gap; then proceeded to Beverly Ford, where it remained until Sept. 16th, thence to Culpepper, remaining there until the 9th of October; again crossing the Rappahannock, it encamped near Beverley Ford, recrossing on the following day, it assisted in driving the enemy, who were advancing back to Brandy Station, the 4th acting as flankers, for the 5th corps. On the 12th the Regiment recrossed the Rappahannock, and fell back with the army, via Bealton, Warrenton Junction, and Centerville, to Fairfax Station, where it remained until the 18th, when it marched forward to Three Mile Station, near Warrenton Junction, and went into camp.

In Col. Lumbard's report. he says : "The Regiment has participated in all the movements of the Army of the Potomac, and have not mentioned the many reconnoisances, and the number of times the Regiment has been on small skirmishes with the enemy. The Regiment has marched during the year over 700 miles."

The 4th, in command of Colonel Lumbard, who had been commissioned as Colonel, to rank from July 3rd, then in 2nd Brigade, 1st Division, 5th Corps, (Griffin's) advanced on the 7th of Nov., 1863, with Army of the Potomac, from its camp near Three Mile Station, on the O. & A. R. R. to the Rappahannock River, and the same day participated in the engagement at Rappahannock Station. On the 3rd the Regiment was ordered, with its Brigade to keep open the communication from Bealton to Kelly's Ford, and engaged in that duty until the 19th, when the command rejoined its corps near Kelly's Ford. Breaking camp on the 26th, the command moved toward the Rapidan River, which it crossed at Germania Ford. On the 28th, the Regiment moved to the right of the position at Mine Run, but did not become engaged. On the night of the 30th, it fell back across the Rapidan. The 5th corps, being ordered on guard duty along the Orange and Alexandria R. R., the Regiment arrived at Bealton on the 1st of December, where it remained until the 30th of April, 1864, when it broke camp and marched to Rappahannock Station. On the 1st of May, the Regiment crossed the Rappahannock River, and camped near Brandy Station, and thence on the 3rd, marched to Culpepper. On the morning of the 4th it started from Culpepper to participate in the Summer Campaign, crossing the Rapidan at Germania Ford. On the 5th, 6th and 7th, the Regiment participated in the Battles of the Wilderness. Col. Lumbard was mortally wounded on the 5th, and died on the 6th. In the same engagement, Capt. W. H. Irvland, Company B, was wounded, and died of his wounds on the 31st of same month. On the night of the 7th, the 4th, then commanded by Lt. Col. J. W.

Hall, moved toward Spottsylvania. Arrived at Laurel Hill on the morning of the 8th, it here became engaged with the enemy, and again on the 9th On the 10th it assisted in a charge upon and capture of the enemy's rifle pits, loosing 20 killed and wounded. On the 11th and 12th the Regiment was in the advanced lines of the corps, and on the 13th and 14th was engaged as skirmishers. On the evening of the latter date the command moved to the left of the army, near Spottsylvania Court House, and remained here until the 19th. It then took part in the movement to North Anna River, which it crossed on the 24th, near Jericho Mills, the Regiment participating in the engagement at this place. On the night of the 26th it recrossed the North Anna and marched to Hanovertown, crossing the Pamunky River on the 28th. On the 29th, 30th and 31st of May, and 1st of June, it was engaged as skirmishers, and on the 3rd it participated in the capture of the enemys line of works near Bethesda church. In the engagement Lieut. James N. Vesey, Company C, was killed. On the 5th, the Regiment marched to Bottoms Bridge, and on the 14th crossed the James River, at Wilcox's Landing, whence it proceeded to the lines in front of Petersburg, where it arrived on the 16th. On the next day the Regiment was engaged as skirmishers, and on the 19th took part in the engagement of that date, loosing 8 killed and wounded. During the engagements from Nov. 1st, 1863, to June 19th, 1864, the Regiment lost 3 officers and 37 men, killed or died of wounds, with 6 missing in action. Although this loss seems small, yet it was about 15 per cent. of its whole strength. The term of service for which the Regiment had been mustered in expired June 19th, 1864. It was accordingly relieved, and on the 20th it embarked on transports at City Point for Washington.

It arrived at Detroit on the 26th, and on the 30th of June the companies were mustered out of service. Of those on the rolls, the terms of 200 men and 23 officers had expired. Of these, 32 men and 1 officer were prisoners, in the hands of the enemy; 135 men and 22 officers were present for muster out, since the 1st of Nov., 1863. The Regiment had received 110 recruits, including a new company, organized at Hillsdale, Michigan, which joined the Regiment on the 16th of May, and which remained in service with the Reorganized Regiment, 129 men of the Regiment re-enlisted as volunteers, and on the 30th of June, there were 280 men and 3 officers on the rolls, whose terms of office had not expired. These were ordered to duty with the First Michigan Infantry, when the 4th left the field of war. The total membership of the 4th Regiment had been, during its service, 1,325, while its losses were 273, of which 8 officers and 115 men were killed in action; 4 officers, 50 men, died of wounds; one officer and 95 men of disease.

> Their brows bear many a gory stain,
> Their white lips press not ours again,
> And eyes that once our life light were.
> Give back a cold, appalling stare.

Reminiscences.

In winter of 1861-2, at Camp Minor's Hill, Virginia, Company B had a man who was an inveterate forager, in fact, he was peculiarly adapted to that branch of service. He would be absent a week at a time. When he showed up

in camp, he was put on extra duty, or punished in some form. At one time he was to stand on a barrel two hours. Some of the boys dug a hole, and placed about a peck of blank cartridges in the same; dug a trench to a tent ten feet away and laid a train of powder; put the barrel over the hole. Soon the culprit was brought, and caused to mount the barrel. Soon that barrel took a flying leap heavenward ten feet in the air. The man, with arms and legs extended, and with a look I never shall forget. When he struck the earth, he said, with a grim sense of humor, " Well boys, you came damned near translating me—making a second prophet of me; I am inclined to think the route you would have caused me to take, would be poor foraging."

On one of his migratorial expeditions, he met with the last enemy to be conquered—Death. He was fairly educated, and a man of good sense. He would not learn drill or to handle a musket. He would have made a proficient spy. I have thought sometimes he was employed in that capacity, unknown to the Regiment, for he would leave camp as soon as he was relieved. The barrel episode was the most severe punishment he ever received, at our hands. It was my province to look after the Company, and absent ones. I rarely reported him absent. I enjoyed many a toothsome viand, the result of his foraging. He had at one time ten thousand dollars, in Erie and Kalamazoo money, and he assured me got rid of it all.

INCIDENT NO. 2.

When the Regiment went into camp for the winter, 1861, the boys built quarters of logs, with canvas tops; Company B built what they called a Hermitage, of timber, mud and canvas. Its capacity was for about twenty of the men. A chimney was constructed of sticks and mud for a base, topped out with barrels. One night, we, of the shoulder straps and high chevrons, got an invite to a barbacue at the Hermitage. As we filed in, a huge fire, with half a yearling steer hanging over the fire place, met our view. It hung directly in the blaze; the boys were occasionally throwing water on the meat to baste it. As fast as the outside was cooked, it was sliced off and passed around. Whiskey was plenty, and copiously used, to wash down the banquet. Songs and speeches were in order. By the way, Company B

had plenty of talent—doctors, lawyers, preachers and gentlemen ; a good time all around. Finally some one of the party, who had not the fear of his Creator, or shoulder straps in his heart, blew up the chimney barrels, and all went up in smoke.

INCIDENT NO. 3.

The writer of this was Orderly Sergeant of Company B a part of 1861-2. And certain characters of the Company considered it legal to plunder this much abused official's pipes, tobacco, and even whiskey was deemed free, whenever or wherever found. The writer suffered many a loss in this line. One especially, who bored him unceasingly for a chance to smoke a very large pipe, holding a quarter pound of tobacco. I will call him "Croxton," "Jack," for short.

One morning I sat in my tent making morning report. I had filled this big pipe, and laid it on the desk in front of me, expecting "Jack" to call for a smoke. He came in due time, and asked if he might smoke my big pipe? I told him I had just filled it for my own use. Well, he said, I was busy

then, and could smoke after he got through. He always had a story to tell me. He sat with his legs hanging inside the doorway, (the shanty was built of logs). I passed him the pipe; he commenced smoking, and telling me a yarn. Soon the pipe exploded, his heels went up, and he over backwards. He arose and said, "you think you are damned smart." He asked for no more smoke.

INCIDENT NO. 4.

One day a blizzard came along, and devastated things generally. Among the calamities was the destruction of our sutlers' shebang. It was in panels, built of thin boards. It was scuttled very promiscuous, and his stock of goods were distributed to all points. The boys were watching with pleased expressions on their countenances. They could stand the temptation no longer, and they went to gathering the spoils in. The sutler howled and ordered them off. They paid no attention. He said he would see about it, and started to see the Colonel. While he was gone, everything in sight was gobbled, and he could not find hide nor hair of

any article. I found two boxes cigars, some figs, a jack knife, and a few other articles, thrust under my tent. I did not hesitate to appropriate, notwithstanding my religious proclivities. It was a clean sweep—a dead loss—to the old boodler. He got my first pay, more than half, and old sledge got the balance. He soon had another invoice of goods, and proceeded to lay up an account against the boys.

INCIDENT NO. 5.

Be it understood, that the calibre of the commission, or officers of the 4th Michigan, was of a high order, for courage and undisputed ability, as the roster in appendix of this narration shows. On a certain occasion, Captain O. was holding a levee at his quarters. All went well. Punch and other refreshments were freely indulged in. Hilarity ran high. Captain O. attempted to make a short speech. His muddled condition caused a remark from another befuddled officer, that did not please the choleric Captain. He threw open the flaps to the entrance of the tent; divested himself of some of his uniform, and proceeded with the attempt to throw his

guests out. But the doughty Captain struck a bigger job than he could handle. The result was, the Captain was picked up and deposited ten rods away in a ditch that had been dug around a tent. This same brilliant officer afterwards commanded a Regiment. He sent them into their first battle without ammunition. But the courage of the promoted Captain was undoubted.

INCIDENT NO. 6.

Fooling with supposed empty shells, is sometimes disastrous. The Banner Company of the Regiment were much given to old sledge and poker, and often plied their avocation into the wee small hours of night, contrary to express orders—lights out after taps. But these injunctions were not always heeded, as the sequel will show. Some of the boys had found a shell not exploded. They, as supposed, dug out all the powder, and on the occasion of a night's occupation of their favorite pastime, used the shell as a candlestick. They inserted their short piece in the fuse hole, and proceeded with the game. The candle burned low; the lighted wick dropped into the shell; a tremendous explosion was the result. It totally demolished the tent, and nearly severed the flag-staff near by—so much so it fell over. But, strange to relate, nobody was hurt. They supposed they had got all the powder out. Moral—do not play cards after taps, nor use a shell for a candlestick, unless you are positive it is not loaded.

INCIDENT NO. 7.

In the spring of 1863, just before the Gettysburg campaign, the 4th Michigan was doing guard duty on the Rappahannock river, at Kelly's Ford, Virginia. The writer's company was detached for picket duty. We were stationed at Mountain Run Ford, down the river from Kelly's Ford, some three miles. The river at this place was shallow. We guarded against cavalry, had to be constantly on the alert.

We also patrolled the river some three miles down. At the end of our patrol rout, lived an old Rebel cuss. He was bitter in his denunciation of the Yankees. His name was Atkinson,—a cousin to the Atkinson of Bleeding Kansas fame. At his house we met another patrol from lower down, and compared notes. We had to watch the old reprobate closely ; also had to keep an eye on his domestics. The first patrol was conducted by the writer, and was quite early in the morning. We followed the bank of the river about a half mile from our reserve. Standing close on the bank of the stream stood a large persimmon tree, well loaded with the luscious fruit. The bank sloped sudden and abrupt from the river. The patrol passed on, and I mounted the tree, crawled out on a big limb, settled myself to scraping in the fruit ; I did not even taste the berries, but dumped them into my haversack. The patrol passed on out of my range. Soon a gentle sound was wafted to my ears from across the river. There was no mistaking the ominous sound and its purport. It said, "Yank! come over." I gazed over the water. There, in plain view, was ten or a dozen rebel cavalrymen, with their carbines pointed at me, and a laughing. They repeated, "Yank, come over." I could see nothing to laugh at, and told them so. They insisted that I should come to them. I told them, "I could not swim, and the water was too deep to wade." Well, "that did not make any difference. You must come anyhow." I said, well, here goes for a try. I slid to the ground. As I struck the earth, one of them fired. The ball went high over my head. I suspect he shot high on purpose to remind me of my obligation.

I waited for no more invitations, but threw myself flat on the ground, and with one tremendous wriggle, slid out of range. This brought a volley from the Rebels. The firing brought my patrol back, double quick. The Rebels skedaddled as fast as their horses could bear them away. The boys were terribly in earnest, but when they knew the situation, they had a big laugh at my expense. The racket also brought our reserve, with a battle in their mind. After learning the cause, the reserve returned, and we, the patrol, went our rounds. The old man Atkinson was the bitterest old devil or Rebel it was my fortune to meet in all my stay in Dixie ; and he did not disguise his sentiments. I will say those persimmons were not ripe ; their looks were deceiving. I advise all who hanker after persimmons, to wait until they are thoroughly ripe ; for unless they are matured, they will pucker up any vacuum that they put their grip upon ; but they are delicious when ripe.

INCIDENT NO. 8.

While the regiment lay at Kelly's Ford, before the Gettysburg campaign, we were paid off. Being in arrear of pay, we received quite a boodle of money. The communication between our army and Washington, by way of Aquia Creek, was temporary and somewhat uncertain. Trains of forage, and ambulances, were sent through attended by a heavy guard. After getting paid, the men were desirious of sending their surplus money home. It would go by Adams' Express, from Aquia. Our chaplain, (Seage,) a brave, good man, volunteered to carry it to Aquia Creek. An ambulance train was going to make the trip, heavily guarded ; the chaplain was to accompany it. The train left very early in the morning without the chaplain. But, nothing daunted, he followed on, expecting soon to overtake it. About four miles out he had to cross a swale with corduroy road. Just across was timber ; and on approaching the timber, he saw two men step from behind trees, and at the same time ordered him to approach. He wheeled his horse, and in turning around one of the would-be robbers fired on him, hitting him in one wrist. This did not stop him. They yelled to him to halt, and at the same time fired again, hitting him in the shoulder. But the knowing mare carried her brave rider to the rear, and out of danger. He threw himself on his faithful horses neck, and clung there until the faithful animal galloped into camp, weak with loss of blood, but with a brave heart still palpitating. A detail of cavalry was immediately sent out, but with no result. Our brave chaplain was kindly cared for, and eventually recovered, but badly crippled. He risked his life to save the boys' money. Our money was returned to us, and we had to carry it through the Gettysburg fight. My share of money sent was four hundred dollars. I had it in my pocket when I was wounded, after, at Gettysburg. I was a prisoner for a few minutes, but the noble Sixth Army Corps made it such a necessity to the Johnnies to git, they had no time to scoop us in. Brave old corps, I remember you with gratitude.

A LITTLE WAR EXPERIENCE.

After the battle of Malvern Hill, our column moved on to Harrison Landing. We arrivied there after daylight, in the morning. Made coffee, and rested a little. The Rebels followed up in small force, and commenced shelling us. We were moved out and formed in line of battle. In front of us was timber ; in our rear was mud, and plenty of it, of a slushy nature. The Rebel guns threw railroad iron at us. They fired high. The missiles went to our rear. As these pieces of iron struck the mud, caused the slush to mount high in air, and in sheets. A New York regiment had just arrived by boat, (a new regiment.) They were moved to our front. I noticed the officers had hand satchels, and had paper collars around their necks. Our fellows cried, "Soft bread," "Fresh fish," and other appellations. The poor devils passed on into the woods, but the Rebels were in full retreat. Hooker had gone out with a brigade, and took them in flank. From here a detail from our regiment was sent to our State to recruit, to help fill the depleted ranks. The writer was one of this number.

We boarded a mail boat that plied between the landing and Fort Monroe, and with an escort, a turtle gun boat, started down the James, for Fort Monroe. On our way down, our boat was the target for Rebel guns along the bank of the river. The pilot house was sheeted over with iron, and when the musket balls came in contact with the iron, it caused a terrible racket. At one place, a bend in the river, they had thrown up a redoubt, and had two pieces of cannon ranged on the river. But our little turtle wiggled up, (gun boat,) and hurled a few shells at them ; causing them to limber up and skedaddle very sudden. We arrived all right at the Fort, took steamer for Baltimore, and to God's country. Recruiting was slow, for the old regiment men feared to enlist for it, as they would be pushed immediately to the front. I would prefer an old organization, as I would get the benefit of their experience. Whereas a new regiment, if pushed to the front, would labor under a great disadvantage.

A LITTLE "BLACK HORSE" CAVALARY, NO TERROR TO 4TH

MICHIGAN BOYS.

A short time before first Bull Run fight, the 4th Michigan, with other regiments, were in camp at Cloud's Mills, Virginia, about 5 miles out from Alexandria, towards Fairfax Court House. Our pickets were well extended out, in above named direction. One day the writer, with about 20 of the Regiment were out towards Fairfax. We seen a small column of cavalry approaching with a flag of truce hoisted. As they drew near, it proved to be an escort of the famous Black Horse Cavalry. We were ranged all along the road as they passed. They were conducting a man and woman to our lines. On their return, we encountered them again. I noticed the contrast between those Rebel troopers, their sullen and vindictive appearance, and compared them to the cheerful and wideawake countenance of our men. They passed on towards Fairfax. We felt we could have cleaned them out in fifteen minutes. There was nothing about the Black Horse

Cavalry, that was very terrifying. I saw better men and horses every day, of our brave troopers.

While the army was stationed along Arlington, from Chain Bridge, Potomac, to Alexandria, Virginia, the 4th Michigan occupied the ground in and about Fort Woodbury, on Arlington. Our picket line was extended out to, or near Minor's Hill, which we occupied, later on, in winter quarters, 1861 2. At one time, while our Regiment was doing guard duty, at above named place, picket firing was in order, with but little damage to either side, but very annoying. One morning, about day break, our doughty and valorous Captain George Spalding, formed about 20 of Company B, and started out to see what could be developed in our front. (By the way, our Captain Spalding was a brave man, a little reckless, but all wool and a yard wide.) We marched out in Indian file, the Captain leading. The writer being 1st Sergeant, was next. After going a half mile, and near the road running down the hill, east, and towards our approach, we saw at our right a picket stationed in a rail pile, put up in Chevron form. He fired his gun, and then took to his heels. Right at the end of the road, where it comes down the hill, the road turned abruptly to the south. Right in this angle the Rebel reserve picket lay. This was also their videt post. About 20 of the Johnnies lay in this elbow, and apparently asleep, for we were within 20 feet of them before they discovered us. The shot of the picket on our approach woke them up. They were taken completely by surprise. They were a good deal excited, (also ourselves,) and broke for their rear. We fired a volley, with some effect. One burley Rebel, ran about ten rods, suddenly halted, turned around, brought his gun to shoulder, and fired. I think the shot was intended for our Captain, but missed him, and I being directly behind him, or a little to his left, the ball just grazed my right ear. Before this Rebel could face to the rear, a shot from the gun of one Fisher, laid him low. Fisher jumped the fence and obtained his knapsack. The racket stired up a nest of Rebels, over the hill. Soon we saw guns dance above the brow of the hill, as the Johnnies double quicked up the slope, on the other side of the hill; they arrived in plain view, battalion front, a whole Regiment of them. Then we were admonished to git —and we did. They fired after us, but without effect. Right here was done some tall skedaddling, through brush, over logs and rough ground. This encroachment on their premises, made the Johnnies mad; they kept up a continual fusillade during the day.

Later on, after going into camp, at Minor's Hill, the Rebels tried to locate a battery about two miles to the west of our camp, and in plain view, a valley between. Two guns of a battery near our head quarters were unlimbered, and proceeded to sling shell over among them. Our fellows greeted them so lively, that the Johnnies were fain to limber up and steal away.

NOTE—The events narrated in these Reminiscences, are not in chronological order, but are facts all the same, as can be verified, and attested by others belonging to the Regiment.

EULOGY.

Comrades, I cannot close this imperfect recital, without saying a few words to you all. I am aware of my inability to do justice to the subject. I have omitted many incidents that happened while in service together. I can see you all as you used to appear on the march, in battle, and in the quiet camp. Your pranks and repartee are fresh in my memory. 45 of the numbers that made up the roster of Company B, were from our sister state, Indiana, and all comrades were true as steel. You all need to be proud of your record, and the part the glorious old 4th took in suppressing treason. A quarter of a century from now will close the roster for nearly all of us ; a much shorter time for myself. Comrades, overlook what you may have seen amiss in me. We are all finite, none perfect. You were a splendid class of men, and none braver. Your record will be handed down to your posterity, and they will point back to your probation here with pride. " My forefathers helped to throttle treason."

GOOD-BY COMRADES.